Clarinet

EASY CHRISTMAS CAROLS
Instrumental Solos

Alfred's Instrumental Easy Play-Along

Contents

	Page	CD Track Demo	Play-Along
Tuning Note (B♭ Concert)			1
Away In A Manger (Medley)	2	2	3
Angels We Have Heard On High	3	4	5
Come, Thou Long-Expected Jesus	4	6	7
Go, Tell It On The Mountain	5	8	9
We Three Kings	6	10	11
It Came Upon The Midnight Clear	7	12	13
Hark! The Herald Angels Sing	8	14	15
Joy To The World	9	16	17
O Come, O Come, Emmanuel	10	18	19
Silent Night	11	20	21
O Come All Ye Faithful	12	22	23
O Little Town Of Bethlehem	13	24	25
The First Noel	14	26	27
What Child Is This?	15	28	29

Arranged by Bill Galliford, Ethan Neuburg and Tod Edmondson

© 2011 Alfred Music Publishing Co., Inc.
All Rights Reserved. Printed in USA.

Alfred Cares. Contents printed on 100% recycled paper.

ISBN-10: 0-7390-8394-5
ISBN-13: 978-0-7390-8394-9

AWAY IN A MANGER (MEDLEY)

Music by
JAMES R. MURRAY (1887) and
WILLIAM J. KIRKPATRICK

Track 2: Demo
Track 3: Play Along

Slowly and gently (♩ = 84)

"Away in a Manger"
Music by JAMES R. MURRAY

"Away in a Manger (Cradle Song)"
Music by WILLIAM J. KIRKPATRICK

© 2011 ALFRED MUSIC PUBLISHING CO., INC.
All Rights Reserved

ANGELS WE HAVE HEARD ON HIGH

Traditional French Melody

COME, THOU LONG-EXPECTED JESUS

Track 6: Demo
Track 7: Play Along

Music by
ROLAND H. PRICHARD

© 2011 ALFRED MUSIC PUBLISHING CO., INC.
All Rights Reserved

GO, TELL IT ON THE MOUNTAIN

Track 8: Demo
Track 9: Play Along

Traditional Spiritual

WE THREE KINGS

Words and Music by
JOHN H. HOPKINS, JR. (1857)

Moderately slow and tenderly (♩ = 180)
(♩. = 60 This represents the song pulse feel counted in one.)

IT CAME UPON THE MIDNIGHT CLEAR

Track 12: Demo
Track 13: Play Along

Music by
RICHARD S. WILLIS

HARK! THE HERALD ANGELS SING

Music by
FELIX MENDELSSOHN

© 2011 ALFRED MUSIC PUBLISHING CO., INC.
All Rights Reserved

JOY TO THE WORLD

Music by
GEORGE F. HANDEL

Moderately slow and gentle (♩ = 72)

O COME, O COME, EMMANUEL

Track 18: Demo
Track 19: Play Along

Music Adapted by
THOMAS HELMORE

Tenderly and flowing (♩ = 120)

© 2011 ALFRED MUSIC PUBLISHING CO., INC.
All Rights Reserved

SILENT NIGHT

Track 20: Demo
Track 21: Play Along

Words and Music by
JOSEPH MOHR and FRANZ GRUBER

© 2009 ALFRED MUSIC PUBLISHING CO., INC.
All Rights Reserved

O COME ALL YE FAITHFUL

Track 22: Demo
Track 23: Play Along

Music by
JOHN FRANCIS WADE

O LITTLE TOWN OF BETHLEHEM

Track 24: Demo
Track 25: Play Along

Music by
LEWIS H. REDNER

© 2011 ALFRED MUSIC PUBLISHING CO., INC.
All Rights Reserved

Track 26: Demo
Track 27: Play Along

THE FIRST NOEL

Traditional English Carol

Track 28: Demo
Track 29: Play Along

WHAT CHILD IS THIS?

Old English Air

PARTS OF A CLARINET AND FINGERING CHART

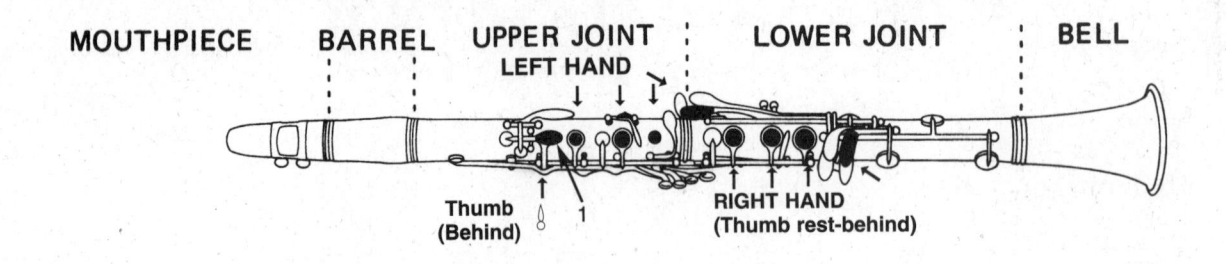

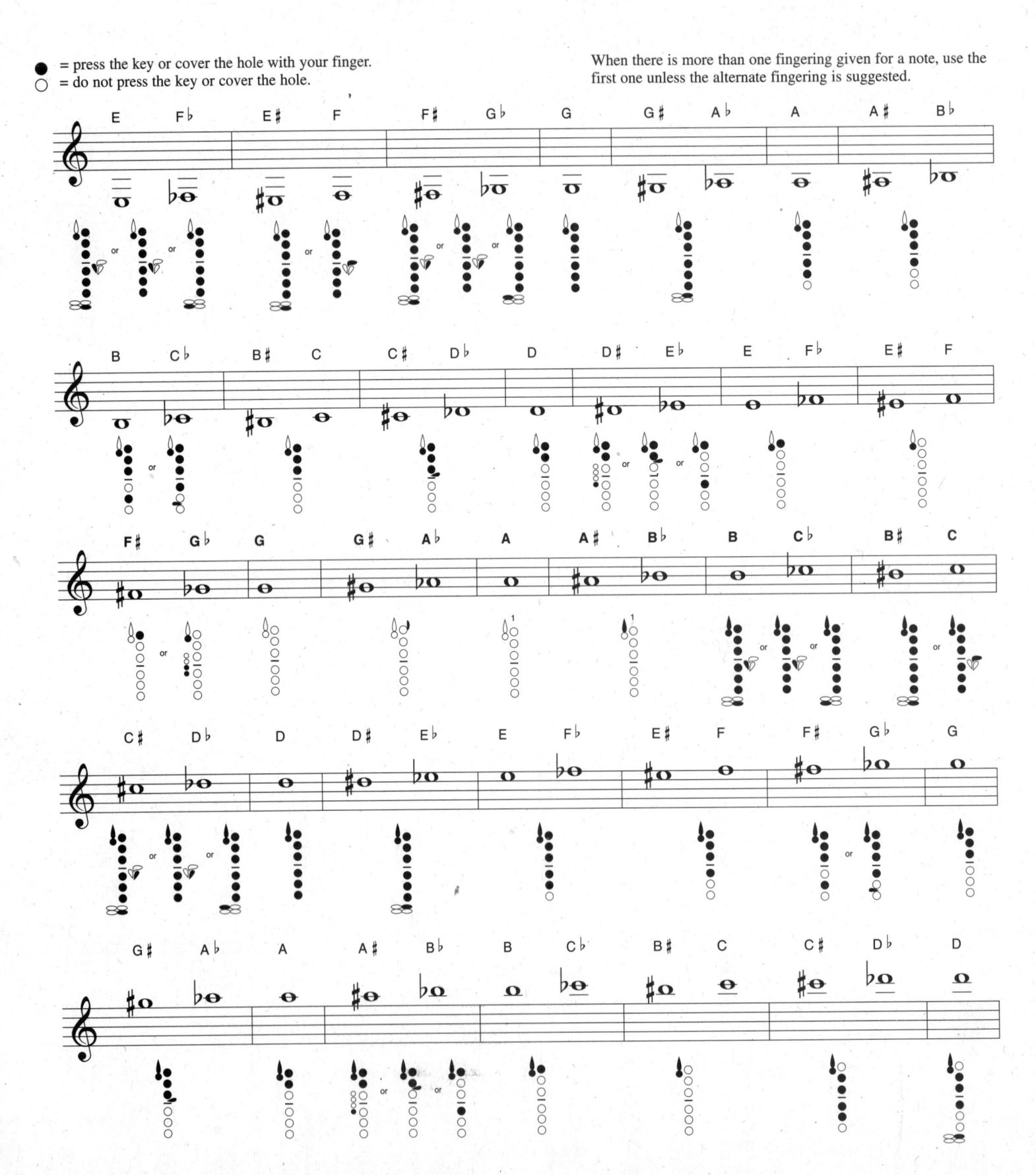